YO-DNN-886

Munchie the Menace
Based on a true story

Written By
Christina Groff-Yoder

Illustrated By
Brooke Lee

ISBN 978-1-7348246-1-2

Table Of Contents

Dedication

AUTHOR'S DEDICATION

This book is dedicated to my mother, Anne Elizabeth Groff, who raised seven children with such love, patience, kindness and compassion. I get my love for children and animals from her. I am the person I am today, because of her unconditional love and guidance. I am very grateful for this and look forward to seeing her again someday in heaven.

ILLUSTRATOR'S DEDICATION

The illustrations in this book are by Brooke Lee and are dedicated in the memory of Kyra Jean Conway, who taught her that she can do anything she puts her mind to, no matter how much she is told otherwise.

CHAPTER 1
A PRESENT FOR GRANDMA

"What are we going to do with that?" said Grandpa.

"I always wanted one of those!" said Grandma.

"Happy Birthday Grandma." "I hope you like her," said Bobby. "I picked her out myself."

"Maaaa," said the goat.

They'd had plenty of pets before, but never a goat. Grandma bent over to pet the goat's back.

The goat busily ate the grass.

"Thank you so much Bobby," Grandma said, giving her grandson a hug.

She felt a tug on her dress. The goat was tasting her dress!

"She likes to nibble on everything!" said Bobby, pulling her away from Grandma's dress. Everyone laughed.

"What should we name her Ma?" said Grandpa.

"Let's see what her personality is like first," said Grandma.

As Grandpa tied her up to the tree in their yard, he wondered if their new pet would be a handful. Little did they know what they were in for.

"Maybe I won't need to mow the grass anymore," Grandpa said, and laughed. Then to their surprise, the goat stood up on her hind legs and started to munch on the leaves overhead.

Grandma smiled and said, "Maybe we should call her Munchie."

CHAPTER 2
THE START OF TROUBLE

After lunch, Grandma and Grandpa went outside to check on their new pet, Munchie, but the goat was gone! She had chewed right through her rope! Grandma and Grandpa started looking all around for her when they heard their neighbor yelling.

"Get out of my garden, you menace!" yelled Mrs. Herman. They saw Mrs. Herman chasing Munchie with a broom.

"You better keep that animal in your own yard!" "It was eating my tomato plants," she told them, sounding upset.

"Maaaa," said Munchie.

"Oh dear, I'm so sorry," said Grandma, leading Munchie home by her collar. "You'll have to build a pen for her Pa," she said.

"Come on, Munchie you menace," Grandpa said, leading the way home.

CHAPTER 3
A PEN FOR MUNCHIE

The next day the grandchildren came to visit. They all laughed when Grandma told them the goat's new name.

"She's a menace already!" said Bobby, the oldest grandchild. "How could a goat be so much trouble?" he asked. *I hope they still want to keep her*, Bobby thought to himself.

Just then, Munchie lowered her head and started pushing Bob's leg with her horns. Bobby stumbled backwards.

"She must want to play," said Bobby.

He started running around the yard. Munchie ran after him, jumping in the air wildly. Munchie enjoyed having the children around to play with.

Bobby helped Grandpa build a nice pen for Munchie. They made her a little stall under the back deck. They put some straw in there for her to sleep on. She rolled in the straw and nibbled it too. She ran and jumped around in her nice, new pen. Out of all the grandchildren, Bobby loved Munchie the most and couldn't wait to come back and see her again.

It was time for him to leave, so he patted Munchie on her head and whispered to her, "Please stay out of trouble, or they might not want to keep you."

"Maaaa," answered Munchie.

CHAPTER 4
THE YELLOW MOUNTAIN

The next day Munchie wandered around her pen munching on grass, when a shiny, yellow car drove up. It was Grandpa's friend. The man went inside. Munchie looked through her fence at the car. It looked nice and high, like one of her favorite places to be. She ran, jumped right over her fence, and up onto the shiny, yellow car! She jumped from roof, to hood, to roof again. Grandpa's friend came running out of the house.

"Get off my car!" he yelled. "I just waxed it!" There were hoof marks all over the car.

"You naughty goat," Grandpa said.

Munchie jumped back over the fence and hid in her stall.

When Bobby came to visit, Grandpa told him about Munchie jumping on the car.

"Yeah, I read that goats like to stand on high places because they are originally from the mountains," Bobby said. "I'm sure she didn't mean any harm." Bobby offered to re-wax the man's car.

Grandpa said, "No, it's okay, but I have

something else you can help me with." Bobby helped Grandpa build Munchie a high platform (not too close to the fence) so she could look all around the yard and be up high the way goats liked to be.

After Grandpa went inside, Bobby whispered to Munchie, "I like to climb on things too," and he giggled. Munchie put her head down and gave Bobby a playful shove with her horns. Bobby took a bag out of his pocket.

"I brought you something," he said. He held out a handful of popcorn and Munchie gobbled it up.

"Maaaa," she said thankfully.

"I thought you would like this," he said, giving her some more.

CHAPTER 5
THE ESCAPE

Munchie liked her new home. She kept the grass in her pen nice and short by munching away at it all the time. From her platform she could reach the tree leaves. So, she munched on them too. Her favorite thing to do was to munch on things. As the days went by, she got fatter.

One day, as Grandma was filling Munchie's water dish, she heard the phone ring. She ran in to answer it, forgetting to shut the gate to Munchie's pen. Munchie pushed the gate open and headed right for Grandma's garden. She looked around the garden. There were all kinds of flowers. She took in a big breath to smell the flowers. The Marigolds smelled delicious. She gobbled them up. Then she ate the Petunias. Then she nibbled on the roses. The thorns didn't even hurt her mouth. A goat's mouth is tough.

After she tasted all the flowers in the garden, she wandered up to the back door of the house. She could hear Grandma talking on the phone in the kitchen. She poked her nose in the cracked screen door and pushed it open. She quietly walked past the kitchen, down the hall. Click, click went her hoofs on the floor. She walked into Grandma and Grandpa's bedroom. She jumped up on the bed and nibbled on the edge of the blanket.

Grandma went into the bedroom and saw Munchie with the fringe of the blanket, dangling from her mouth. She chased her back outside, waving her arms in the air, running after her. Then she saw her flower garden.

"Oh Munchie, you menace," she said, shaking her head. Grandma locked her back in her pen. "You need to stay out of trouble."

CHAPTER 6
THE CAMP OUT

Bobby often came to visit his grandparents and Munchie. On Friday, he brought Grandma some flowers to make up for the ones Munchie ate. He hoped that Grandma would still love Munchie, even though she ate some flowers. Bobby's friend, Jim came along that day too. They were going to have a camp out. Once they had the tent up in the yard next to Munchie's pen, they brought her out to play. When Munchie saw the big tent, she ran and jumped on top of it. It came crashing down on top of her.

"Maaaaaaaa!" she cried, trying to find her way out of the tangled mess. Bobby and Jim laughed and laughed. They thought she sounded surprised that she wasn't standing triumphantly on top of the tent.

"Silly goat, you can't stand on a tent," said Bobby. Then they had a lot of fun playing chase with Munchie before it was time to put her back in her pen and set the tent back up.

CHAPTER 7
WASH DAY

The next day was Saturday. Grandma always hung the clothes out on the line to dry on Saturdays. Bobby carried the big basket of wet clothes over to the line for Grandma. Munchie sniffed the air and watched them closely.

"Maaaa," said Munchie.

"Good morning Munchie," said Grandma.

Grandma pinned up the clothes, one piece at a time with the clothes pins. She liked the way they smelled after they dried in the sun. The clothes blew in the breeze.

Munchie sniffed the air again. She wandered over to the fence. She jumped up and put her two front legs on the fence so she could stretch her neck out further. Grandma's night gown was blowing towards the fence. She reached out, stretching as far as she could, and grabbed the edge of the night gown with her lips. She pulled it and nibbled at it.

"No, no, don't eat Grandma's clothes," Bobby

said as he pushed her down off the fence. "I'm sorry, Grandma."

"It's okay Bobby," "It's not your fault, Munchie has a big appetite," said Grandma, pinning the gown up higher.

CHAPTER 8
THE PET SHOW

The next week, Bobby called his Grandma on the phone. He was excited to tell her about a pet show that he'd heard about.

"Grandma, there's a pet show today at four o'clock," "Can we enter Munchie in it please?" "I know she'll win!" he said. *Maybe if she wins, Grandma will be proud of her*, Bobby thought.

"Settle down," said Grandma. "Okay, we can put her in the back of the truck and come pick you up around three."

"Oh great!" "I can't wait!" said Bobby, jumping up and down.

The time flew by faster than Bobby thought it would and soon they were on their way to the show. Bobby led Munchie in by her leash. There were all different kinds of pets. There were puppies, kittens, guinea pigs, rabbits, and a few birds in cages. But Munchie was the only goat. Bobby was sure she would win first place.

Bobby and Munchie sat behind a little boy wearing a baseball cap. He held a small dog in his lap. Of course, Munchie decided to take a nibble of the boy's hat. The boy's puppy started barking at Munchie.

"Stop that, Munchie," Bobby said, pulling the hat

out of her mouth and giving it back to the boy. "Sorry about that."

The boy just giggled and put his hat back on his head. The puppy wagged its' tail. It wanted to play with Munchie, but she was too busy looking around for something she could munch on next.

The judges walked around and looked at all the animals. Bobby proudly held Munchie's collar as the judge asked him questions about his pet. He was so excited to be there; he could hardly sit still. He hoped Munchie would win a ribbon. The prizes were soon ready to be announced.

"The winner in the category for the cutest pet goes to…" announced a judge. A furry little kitten won that ribbon. *Well, that kitten is really cute*, thought Bobby. The second category was for the most playful pet. The playful little puppy who belonged to the boy with the baseball cap, won that ribbon. The third category was for the funniest pet. Bobby held his breath. *Munchie is funny*, thought Bobby. A little girl in blue overalls, was so proud of her guinea pig that she bounced up to the judges' table to receive the prize.

By this time, Munchie was getting restless. She spotted some bright red and blue ribbons on a table. She headed that way, pulling Bobby behind her.

"Where are you going?" cried Bobby, trying to hold her back. Munchie started running, knocking over little children as she went. Bobby lost hold of her leash and she jumped up on the judges' table. Little kids giggled, laughed and pointed at her. Munchie started nibbling on the prize ribbons. Bobby finally caught up to her and tried to pull her down off the table. He was worried that Grandma would not love her any more after causing so much ruckus.

The startled judge said, "Looks like she's claimed that ribbon."

"The one for the biggest trouble maker!" yelled a kid in the crowd.

Everyone laughed and agreed, so Munchie was nominated for the prize. The judge pinned the

big blue ribbon on Munchie's collar. The one with some bites out of it. Grandma made her way over to the stage. She smiled and laughed. She leaned over, patted Munchie on the head and said, "We all love you, even if you are a trouble maker." Bobby knelt down beside Munchie and threw his arms around her neck to hug her. He was so happy to know that Grandma loved her, even though she hadn't won first place.

ABOUT THE AUTHOR

Christina Groff-Yoder earned an associate's degree in Communication and Liberal Arts from Harrisburg Area Community College and had her poems and short stories published in 2003, 2004 and 2005 H.A.C.C. Lancaster Campus Literary Journals. She and her husband have raised seven children over the years and have had plenty of pets, including goats. She now has five grandchildren and resides with her husband, Evan, in Lancaster County, Pennsylvania.

ABOUT THE ILLUSTRATOR

Brooke Lee lives in Nevada. She was self-employed at age nineteen and opened her very own business at the age of twenty one. Dedicated to working, Brooke is a pet stylist by day and pursuing her lifelong love of creating art at night. Her best friend is a Pug and her biggest dream is to work for a video game company someday. You can contact Brooke Lee at brooke.lee.96@gmail.com.

Made in the USA
Las Vegas, NV
12 November 2021

34228400R00017